hamsters

understanding and
caring for your pet

Written by
Dr Anne McBride BSc PhD Cert.Cons FRSA

hamsters

understanding and
caring for your pet

Written by
Dr Anne McBride BSc PhD Cert.Cons FRSA

Magnet & Steel Ltd

www.magnetsteel.com

Printed and bound in South Korea.

ISBN: 978-1-907337-04-8
ISBN: 1-907337-04-0

Contents

Perfect pets

Golden, or Syrian hamsters make delightful pets and have been popular with families for many years.

There are lots of reasons why hamsters are attractive animals to keep:

- If treated gently, they rarely bite and like to interact with their owners.

- Hamsters are not expensive to buy or to keep.

- They are clean creatures and, providing they are kept well, they do not smell.

- Hamsters are small, with males weighing between 85– 130 g (3– 4.5 ozs) and females between 90– 150 g (3– 5 ozs), so they do not need a lot of space, compared to other pet animals such as rabbits, guinea pigs, dogs and cats.

- Syrian hamsters come in a range of different colours and coat types.

- They are happy to live on their own, so you only need to keep one.

Special requirements

Syrian hamsters are lots of fun, with their rounded bodies and inquisitive nature. But, like all animals, they have their own specific needs which you need to know about before buying your first hamster. This is important so you can have a good relationship with your hamster, and it can live a long, healthy and happy life. If you are buying the hamster for a child, please remember that it is still the adult's responsibility to ensure your pet is well cared for and properly handled.

- You will need to handle your hamster gently, as they are easily frightened, especially when picked up. For this reason, young children should be supervised.

- You need to give your hamster the right food to stay fit and healthy.

- Long haired hamsters will need grooming every day.

- You will need to clean out your hamster's home regularly.

- You need to provide a cage that is large enough for them to exercise properly. Hamsters are very energetic and must have appropriate things to do to keep them occupied.

- Syrian hamsters are most active at night, and find bright lights and noise distressing.

- You will need to make arrangements for someone to look after your hamster if you go away on holiday.

- You will need to check over your hamster every week to ensure it is healthy.

- You will need to commit to looking after your hamster throughout its life, which may be 2 years.

What is a Syrian hamster?

Hamsters are members of the rodent family. This is the largest group of mammals, and contains over 2,000 different species of varying shapes and sizes. The word rodent comes from the Latin word 'rodere', to gnaw, and gnawing is one thing all rodents have in common. They gnaw to get their food and to make their homes. Rodents have four big front teeth, the incisors, that are evolved for gnawing. These sharp chisel-shaped teeth meet together like pincers and are very effective. They grow continually throughout the animal's life.

There are over 50 species and sub-species of hamster in the world. The Syrian or Golden hamster has some close cousins that you may also see in the pet shop. These are Dwarf hamsters, most commonly the Russian and Roborovski species. However, there is a major difference between them. While dwarf hamsters enjoy each other's company, Syrian hamsters are purely solitary animals, true loners. This means they must be kept on their own. Keeping two Syrian hamsters together, even if they are from the same litter, or the opposite sex, will most certainly cause a lot of stress and fighting. They will fight mostly at night, and can cause serious injury to each other and even death.

Syrian hamsters, as their name suggests come from a small part of Northwest Syria, in the Middle East. Unfortunately there are very few left in the wild. This sad state of affairs is also the case for their much larger European cousin. The European hamster (Cricetus cricetus) is the size of a Guinea pig and is native to Western Europe, where it used to be regarded as an agricultural pest. Due to extensive pest control measures and changes in the crops we now grow, there is little habitat left that is suitable for these impressive creatures. They are now so rare in the wild that the species is regarded as critically endangered. It has rather an aggressive nature and is not kept as a pet.

The Syrian hamster's official latin name is *Mesocricetus auratus*, a very long name for such a little creature. It is more correct to call them Syrian rather than Golden hamsters because there is now a wide variation in coat colours available, not just the original wild type golden coat. They belong to a family of rodents called the Myomorpha, which also includes mice, rats, gerbils, lemmings and voles. The word hamster comes from the German word 'hamstern' meaning to hoard. This very accurately describes a major behaviour of these animals.

The hamster's natural environment is the dry rocky areas and scrubby slopes of the mountains around Aleppo. They live in deep burrows which each individual constructs as its own home. These burrows are about 200 cm (80 inches) long and 65 cm (30 inches) deep and have several tunnels and chambers. They stay in these cool burrows during the day, thus avoiding the heat and dryness of the surface. Hamsters quickly overheat and will die at temperatures of 36°C (97°F). Hamsters are very tidy creatures and will use different parts of their burrow system for different activities. One part will be used as a latrine (toilet), another for their food larder and another for their sleeping and resting area, where they will spend long periods of time grooming, keeping their coat very clean. A female will use yet another part as a nursery for her babies.

Members of the rodent family: Gerbils (top) Rats (centre) and Hamster (bottom).

Hamsters are exceptionally busy animals. They are active at night when they come out of the burrows to search for food and explore their world, clean their sleeping area and make a new nest. They will also repair and extend their old burrow or dig a new one. They are very curious creatures and will climb over rocks, dig tunnels and gather food in their specially adapted mouths.

The hamster's mouth has cheek pouches that extend along the jaw, almost back to the shoulders. They are lubricated by mucus which enables the hamster to push food along to the back, a bit like you filling up your shopping bag. They can carry almost half their weight in these pouches – similar to a human carrying 30 kilos (70 lbs), in their mouth! They gather food and nesting material and carry it back in their strong mouth pouch to the safety of their burrow. Hamsters store their food in a pile from which they can eat later in peace and safety. They are omnivores. This means their natural diet includes meat, in the form of insects and grubs, as well as seeds, nuts and fruit.

Hamsters are very active animals and can run at speeds of 8 km (5 miles) an hour. They can travel long distances in their search for food, climbing over rocks and wandering through the scrub.

They are not sociable animals and will be aggressive to each other when they meet. There are two exceptions to this; when a male and female come together to mate, and when a female is rearing her babies. She can have as many as 11 in a litter. Baby hamsters are born hairless and their eyes and ears are closed, so they do not see or hear. They do, however, have a sharp set of teeth when they are born. Their ears open when they are about 4 days old and the eyes at about 2 weeks and the hair begins to grow about a week after birth. At this stage they are totally dependent on their mother to keep them fed, warm and protected. They start to eat solid food and drink water when they are about 10 days old and are weaned around three weeks of age, when the mother starts to leave them to look after themselves for periods of time by making a separate nest to sleep in. Around two weeks of age the babies start to play fight. However, this sociable period of their life is short lived and, two weeks later, when they are one month old they are sexually mature and the fighting is no longer play but serious. At this time they disperse, going off to make their own burrows and fend for themselves.

It is important to realise that hamsters are prey animals and are a major source of food for many predators.

They are hunted on the ground by animals and from the air by birds. This has an effect on everything they do and is why they are continually on the alert and are very nervous. Hamsters are very adept at spotting danger. They have excellent hearing and sense of smell and, while quite short sighted, the position of their eyes means they can see above as well as behind them. They run away to safety at the first sign of any danger.

The human link

The history of the relationship between hamsters and humans is fascinating and unusual. They were first brought to the attention of the West by Alexander and Patrick Russell who described them in their book 'The Natural History of Aleppo' in 1756.

However a real hamster was not seen in England until 1839, when George Waterhouse, a British naturalist, returned from his travels with the skull and skin of a golden hamster. He took it to the Zoological Society of London where it was classified and given its Latin name. Forty years later a retired gentleman, James Henry Skeene, kept a small colony at his home in Edinburgh. Few others were interested in these little animals and, after 30 years, this rather inbred colony died out.

However, in the 1930s, three or four baby hamsters (some suggest it was as many as eleven individuals), all from the same litter, were taken from the wild and successfully bred in the Hebrew University in Jerusalem. Some of their young were brought to Britain. Though a few more wild hamsters were caught in 1971, 1978 and 1982, these animals did not form part of the colony from which our pet hamsters are derived. It is amazing to think that the millions of hamsters kept around the world, in all their varieties, are all descended from fewer than a dozen individuals and have only been pets for some 70 years.

The hamster's world

The hamster's world

Find out how a hamster functions and how it sees the world.

Nose

Hamsters rely on smell to identify each other, find food, and to detect the scent of a nearby predator. They can recognise other hamsters and different people just by scent.

Whiskers

These are extremely sensitive and are used to help the hamster find its way in the dark and as a measure to decide whether it can fit through a space or if the ground drops away in front of it. The hamster is unique in the mobility of its whiskers.

When the hamster is resting, they are flat and still, when alert the whiskers remain still but are raised to stick out from its face. However, when the hamster is exploring or investigating some new object, the whiskers sweep back and forth.

Mouth

As already described, the hamster's mouth has large cheek pouches used for carrying food and bedding material back to its burrow.

Teeth

Hamsters have 16 teeth that grow all the time and need to be worn down if it is not to suffer from painful dental conditions. They need to be given the right food and appropriate things to gnaw, like untreated fruit tree wood.

Eyes

Hamsters have panoramic vision, seeing behind them, to the sides and above their head, but not right in front of the nose. Their eyes are adapted for seeing at twilight and night when light levels are low. Bright light, such as sunshine and electric lights, are painful to hamsters.

Hamsters are very short sighted, so it is best to talk to them gently when you approach them so as to not startle them. If you do startle them, they may well bite because they are afraid.

Hamsters have red or black eyes.

Ears

Like other rodents, hamsters hear far better than us. They can hear high pitched sounds which we cannot, in the ultra-sonic range. This means they hear noises from human equipment such as televisions and refrigerators. For hamsters these are very loud and stressful and they will need a quiet place to live in your home.

Feet

The front feet have four claws (nails) and there are five on the back feet. The soles of the feet are bare and very sensitive, like our hands and fingers. The front toes are used for holding food, gripping surfaces as they climb and for grooming their coat.

Movement

Hamsters walk, trot and run. They can squeeze through narrow gaps. If their head can get through then so can the rest of their body.

Tail

Hamsters have a very short tail which they use to help them balance when they are climbing or standing up on their back legs.

Body

The body is compact and pear shaped, with strong muscles on the hips and shoulders.

Coat

The coat may be short or long. It may be a single colour, mixture or have special markings depending on the type of hamster. There is even a hairless variety!

Coat varieties

Wild Syrian hamsters are golden brown with a pale, off-white belly. They have dark patches on the cheek with off-white crescents behind. However, by breeding particular individuals together hamster fanciers have produced over 40 different coat colours and three types of coat textures. A huge range when you remember how few animals formed the original breeding group back in 1930. You may wish to have a particular variety, especially if you wish to show your pet.

Pictured; Golden hamster (left) Black Banded hamster (centre) and Chinese hamster (right).

Colours & marking

Coat colours are divided into three types: agouti, self coloured and patterned.

Agouti

There are two colours in this type; golden and cinnamon.

Golden

This ranges from a light golden yellow colour (like syrup) to deep mahogany red. The belly is light coloured, and there may be darker patches on the chest and back. The golden colour is that of the original wild hamsters.

Cinnamon

This is one of the oldest varieties of hamster, dating back to the 1950s and commonly found in pet stores. As the name suggests, the coat is a bright orange-brown overlaid with lighter coloured hairs. The eyes are red but darken with age.

Pictured; Satin Golden hamster

Self coloured

These hamsters are the same colour all over and have no darker cheek patches. They usually have a white stripe under their chin and a white patch on their chest or belly. There are several varieties which include:

Dark-eared white

This hamster is a partial albino with red eyes, a white coat, but dark grey ears.

Black

First bred in the 1980s this is a fairly new colour, and these hamsters look like they are dressed up for a ball, in their black suit, white shirt and shoes! Essentially black with a dashing white stripe under the chin and white around the feet.

Black-eyed cream

This has a cream coloured coat, which may be sandy coloured or have a rich orange tone. It has black eyes and ears.

Sable

This was first bred around 1975. The hair roots are cream and the tops range from charcoal grey to very dark brown or black. There are enchanting cream rings around the dark eyes. Young Sables are almost black but the coat lightens as they grow.

Pattern

These hamsters have coats of more than one colour.
Different varieties include:

Banded

These are distinguished by the band of white just
behind the front legs that circles right around the
body. The rest of the coat can be any of the standard
colours.

Piebald

The coat has irregular patterns of colour all over.

Tortoiseshell

Like Tortoiseshell cats, these hamsters have red and
black blocks of coloured hair.

Coat type

Short Hair or Fancy: this coat resembles that of the original wild stock.

Long hair or teddy

This coat needs extra care and the hamster needs grooming every day to prevent mats and tangles. The females tend to have a fluffy coat, whilst the males can have coats over 7 cm (3 inches) long.

Rex

These are not usually found in pet stores. The coat has a velvety look and feel.

All three coat types also come in Satin. This has a sheen to it which is due to the hair reflecting more light. It does this because each strand is thinner and has more air pockets in it than normal hamster hair, creating a more reflective surface.

Hairless

As with all hamster colour and coat varieties, the hairless hamster is a result of breeding from animals with genetic mutations. However, these Hamsters are rare and have a shorter life expectancy than those with hair. They also need special care and are not advised as pets.

Setting up
home

Setting up home

Before you buy your hamster, you will need to decide where you are going to keep it, then buy suitable housing and get it ready before you bring your pet home. Hamsters do not tolerate heat and should be kept away from sunny windows and radiators and, of course draughts. Ideally the room temperature should be between 18- 26°C (65- 79°F).

Remember hamsters are highly sensitive to sound, and frightened of sudden noises. Their home should be in a quiet part of the house.

They do not like bright lights, so find somewhere in a darker corner of a room for their home.

- Your hamster's home should be as big as possible. They are very active and like space to run around and explore.

If their home is small they may become stressed, as they have too little to do. The accommodation will need to contain a dark, draught free sleeping area.

- You can buy a specially-made cage. The most common types have bars on the sides and top. You can attach toys and a wheel to these as well as shelves for your hamster to climb on. Do not buy cages with wire floors or wire shelves as these can hurt your hamster's feet.

You can also buy modular cages, with tunnels that interconnect, rather like a hamster's burrow. These need to have adequate ventilation in the tunnels. You can have fun adding to your hamster's home with new tunnels, or changing their arrangement, giving your pet new routes to explore.

- The bottom of the cage should be covered with at least 2 inches of bedding. This allows your hamster to dig, and soaks up any mess.

- Suitable materials for digging, burrowing and bedding should be paper based and include shredded tissue paper or paper towels, or torn up paper and newspaper. Paper based bedding materials are easily found in pet stores. Meadow hay is also excellent bedding material.

Wood shavings and sawdust are easily available and cheap, but not advised as they can contain chemicals and dust that can cause breathing problems for your hamster. Likewise, any other dusty materials, such as cat litter, should be avoided.

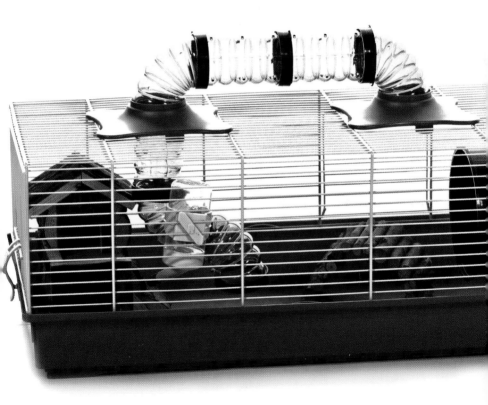

Materials that are fibrous such as cotton wool (cotton), wood wool or any synthetic materials should not be used. They can easily cause injury to your hamster by getting tangled around feet or teeth or swallowed, causing impaction of the gut which can be fatal.

- When you add new bedding, pile it up in the middle of the cage. This way your hamster can be occupied as it arranges its home to its own satisfaction.

- You may want to provide your hamster with an even deeper area to burrow in. An area with a solid floor filled with deep bedding has been shown by scientists to be very important to hamster welfare. If the whole cage is not suitable then provide them with a large, deep plastic box in part of their accommodation as a digging pit. Fill the box with a mixture of sand and soil. The sand should be the type used for children's sandpits and the soil sterilised. This is easily done by heating it in a microwave. Make sure it is completely cool before you put it in your hamster's digging pit. You will need to provide a ramp so your hamster can get in and out of the box easily.

Pictured; Golden hamster

- Attach a water bottle to the side of the cage. A bottle is better than a bowl as water bowls can quickly be soiled with food and bedding, or tipped over, making your hamster's home damp.

- Because hamsters are clean animals, they can easily be toilet trained. Your hamster will choose the part of its home it thinks suitable as a toilet area for urinating. You will know where this is by the soiled bedding or by the white crust formed from the dried urine. In this spot, place a jam jar on its side with some clean bedding and a little soiled bedding in it. This tells the hamster that this is its new toilet. The jar should be cleaned regularly, at least weekly, and replaced as necessary.

- Ensure your hamster's home is safe from other pets, such as cats and dogs, and that he has places to hide if he feels scared.

When you take your hamster out of the cage do be very careful. They are quick to escape and not easy to recapture!

- You should have a dedicated play pen area that is blocked off so that your hamster cannot escape under the furniture, or even under the floor boards! The play pen area should have a dark box or tunnel that your hamster can use as a safe hiding place if it feels scared.

Playtime

Hamsters should be given the chance to behave naturally. They are inquisitive animals and in the wild would tunnel through the grass, climb over rocks, dig burrows and forage for food.

All hamsters should be given lots of bedding and appropriate toys to play with, to give them both physical and mental stimulation. You may even wish to teach them tricks.

Teaching tricks can be a great way of bonding with your hamster and is lots of fun (see further reading). They can be taught to come when called, go back to their cage on cue, even retrieve tiny objects.

You can help your hamster to live a full life by doing the following:

- Give them toys made of natural, untreated wood. Fruit tree twigs are ideal. Wooden toys made for parrots are also suitable.

- Do not give hard, plastic toys. When your hamster chews them they can splinter and leave sharp edges. Also, if a hamster swallows a fragment it may become extremely ill.

- Make hiding places from cardboard boxes or the cardboard centres of toilet rolls. These can be empty or you can put bedding and some food in them, giving your pet the chance to rummage among the bedding for some tasty treats and chew up the cardboard box, real hamster heaven.

- Pet shops also sell wooden bridges and rodent playgrounds which you can use to help keep your hamster fit either in the cage or when you take it out.

- Provide your hamster with a wheel. This should have a solid back and sides, but not an exposed spindle. It should fit to the side of the cage. An alternative is the 'flying saucer' wheels that are free standing, slightly dish-shaped and tilted at a 45 degree angle. Do not get one that is too small. If your hamster has to curve its spine when standing in it, he will do long term-damage to hips, shoulders and back.

- Hamster exercise balls are also known as globe balls. These are plastic balls into which you put the hamster and it can move the ball around the room. Some are fitted to a track. Whichever you choose, they need to be used with extreme caution. While it can be lots of fun to watch your hamster roll around the room and even somewhere to put it while you clean out its home, it is very easy for your hamster to get the ball stuck in a small space or roll down stairs and injure itself.

Bowls

You will need at least two bowls – one for food and one for water – though four are ideal, so you can wash one set while another set is being used. Choose from plastic, ceramic or stainless steel. In the long-term, the last two are better options, as plastic bowls can scratch eventually and become quite abrasive.

The design is important: cats prefer to eat from shallow bowls rather than deep ones.

Food

Find out in advance what the kitten is fed, so you can get a supply before you bring him home.

Litter accessories

Your kitten should not be allowed outside until he's at least six months old, so you will need a litter tray, scoop, poo bags/nappy sacs (for depositing the poop), cat-safe disinfectant for cleaning, and a supply of cat litter. Even when he is allowed to go outside, you'll still need a tray for night-time use. Cats shouldn't be allowed out after dusk and before dawn for their own safety (they are most at danger of road accidents when it's dark).

If you already have a cat, do still get another tray for the newcomer, as it is recommended that there is one tray per cat. For indoor house cats, who don't go outside, add another extra tray still – so two cats will need three trays between them.

A covered tray, whether with an open front or a cat-flap front, will help to control odours. Some even have filters in the top of the tray. Some kittens prefer the privacy that a covered tray offers, while others can feel claustrophobic and prefer a standard 'open' tray. Do bear in mind that the best way of keeping a sweet-smelling home is to scoop regularly and to change the entire litter regularly – whether the tray has a cover or not. If the litter is very dirty, most cats won't use it and will find a clean corner of the house to relieve themselves instead!

There are many types of litter – wood-based pellets, paper, clay, silica crystals, lightweight, and the type that forms a scoopable clump when it comes into contact with water. Find out what your kitten is used to and get a supply before bringing him home. If you want to change the type of litter, add a little of the new material to the one he's used to already, mix it in, and gradually, over the course of a few days, increase the amount of new to old until a complete change-over has been achieved.

Tip: If your kitten is fussy about the type of litter he uses, try a fine grain, which many cats prefer.

Identification

Most rescue centres will microchip the animals in their care before they are rehomed, but if you get your kitten from another source, then you may have to arrange for your vet to do it. It is a simple procedure where a small chip, the size of a long grain of rice, is inserted under the skin at the back of the neck, between the shoulder blades. This chip contains a unique number, which will be held on a database with your details. If your kitten becomes lost and is scanned by a reader, you can quickly be reunited. Occasionally, chips fail or migrate, so it is worth asking your vet to scan your cat at his annual check-up, to ensure it's still working properly, but the failure rate is very low and chipping has proved to be a very easy, reliable form of identification.

In addition, a collar and tag is useful so your kitten can be returned to you without a scanner and if it is made of reflective material, it could help improve your kitten's visibility in low light.

It is very important that the collar is a safe one and will not strangle your kitten if it is caught on a branch or something similar. A safety-clip collar that snaps open under pressure is a good option.

Scratching post

Scratching is an important part of feline behaviour. Expecting a kitten not to scratch is entirely unreasonable, but scratching needn't be a problem – as long as you provide him with suitable places to scratch. If he has a scratching post in your lounge, placed at the right height and in the right position, then he'll have no need to put his claws anywhere near your new sofa. Two or three posts should be sufficient for most homes, but you may need more if you have more than one cat, especially if they don't go outside very much.

Avoid carpet-covered scratching boards and posts – your kitten might associate the material with the action and then begin scratching your floor-coverings. Sisal is therefore preferable.

Toys

A good selection of toys is vital. If you spend time regularly playing with your kitten, you will not only strengthen your relationship, but you'll also be helping to keep him active and stimulated (if bored, he will seek amusement by climbing your curtains, 'hunting' your shoelaces etc). Plus, playing with a kitten is simply great fun and a fabulous way of de-stressing!

The range of toys available these days is astonishing, with everything from fishing-rod type toys and balls with bells to remote-controlled mice and multi-toy activity centres. There is something to suit every puss – and purse!

Whatever toys you buy, don't make every one constantly available to your kitten. To keep his interest in them, put them away, and bring out a couple every day for him to play with. The next day, swap them with different toys. Rotating his toys will help to retain their novelty value for longer.

Also remember that toys don't play themselves. Giving him a toy mouse might amuse him for a few minutes, but he'll soon lose interest if it's not wiggled to attract his attention, or thrown for him to chase and 'hunt'.

Feliway

Scent is very important to cats and kittens, not only as a means of communication to other cats but also in terms of his own personal sense of security. If a home smells of his own odour, he will feel far safer than in a new home where there are unfamiliar scents. Kittens put their own smells on objects by rubbing their scent glands against them, particularly facial glands. This is why a kitten will rub his head against the side of furniture, your legs, or against your hand while he is being petted.

Before you bring your new kitten home, put a pheromone diffuser (Feliway) in his room and leave it on continuously for at least four weeks. This will reassure him and really help him to feel secure and 'at home'.

Sexing

You can tell the sex of your hamster by looking under its rear end. Males are sexually mature around four to five weeks of age and will have a lump where the testicles are. It is normal for these to be quite large in hamsters. Younger animals can be identified as male or female by the distance between the anus and the genitalia. In females the two are close together, while in males there is a noticeable gap.

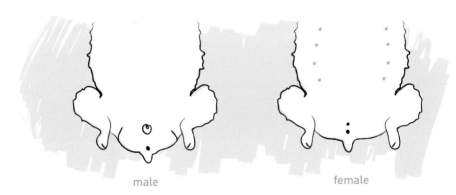

male   female

Making friends

Though hamsters are naturally curious animals, they are easily frightened and will be anxious when they first come to live with you.

If you spend time getting to know your hamster, it will stop being frightened of you and become very tame. For the first couple of days, your hamster needs peace and quiet to settle into its new home. You will need to provide food and change the water, so he can start getting used to you, without the stress of being handled. You can even train him to come to you when called. Start this by whistling or saying his name softly and tap on the cage gently before you put the food down. He will soon learn that your voice and his name mean something pleasant.

Handling

Hamsters naturally waken around dusk and go to sleep, around dawn. They are most active after dark, but you can teach a hamster to get used to getting up in the late afternoon or early evening by waking it up at the same time every day for petting, grooming and playtime. If your hamster is asleep, then wake it gently, or it will be disorientated, stressed and rather fearful. Wake your hamster by talking to it and gently rustling its bed with your finger or a pencil. Once it is awake give it a minute or two to get its bearings before you try to handle it.

When your hamster appears to be awake, happy and relaxed, you can start making friends.

- To begin with, come close to the cage and talk to it. Do not make any sudden movements.

- Offer treats so the hamster has to come up to see you and get used to your hand. Hold your hand quite still and let the hamster sniff your fingers and hand. If you move suddenly you are likely to scare it and you may get nipped as it panics and runs away.

- The next stage is to put some food on the palm of your open hand and let your hamster walk on to your hand to get the treat. When it is happy to do this, gently place your other hand over its back, lift it out of the cage and bring it to your chest.

- Use the same technique to put your hamster back in its cage.

- Do not scoop or grab your hamster from above. From the hamster's point of view this sudden movement means it is being attacked by a predator, it will be very frightened and is highly likely to bite you.

- Likewise, do not hold your hamster by the loose skin at the scruff of the neck, this is painful and again, the hamster will tell you by biting. They can wriggle and are agile, and may turn and bite your fingers.

Do not turn your hamster on its back and stroke his tummy. He will lie very still, because this is a very scary position for him – he is playing dead. It will lie still because it is trying to pretend to be dead and thus of no interest to a predator. It will remain like this until it thinks the scary thing has gone away, such as when you move your hands away. This is a common behaviour in many small animals. Do not be fooled that he is relaxed or in a trance. He will be alert and stressed, and when he thinks it is safe to do so he will suddenly try to escape and may injure himself.

Other pets

If you have other pets, such as a dog, cat or ferret, you will need to be very careful. You should never allow other pets near without supervision. Dogs, cats, ferrets and snakes are meat-eaters and you would not want your hamster to end up as their tasty snack.

Food glorious food

A well-balanced diet will keep your hamster healthy, and will help to ensure a good, long life. In the wild, they eat grass, plants, roots, seeds, berries and insects, and will even eat some meat if they find a carcase. It is essential that they eat a lot of hard foods that help keep their teeth in good shape.

Complete foods

There are several varieties of hamster feed available in pet stores some are mixes that look a bit like human muesli; others are pellets or blocks.

Mixes

These are particularly good for hamsters as they can nibble at different bits as their fancy takes them. Do check your pet's hoard of food every week, if it is too big it means you are feeding too much, and your hamster may only be eating his favourite bits and not be getting a balanced diet.

Be careful of buying the cheap, 'budget' brands as these may not have the correct proportions of protein and fats for your pet, or contain mixed animal protein rather than from a particular type of animal. A good mix will contain seeds, nuts, dried fruit and grains and some animal protein (usually chicken). They may come pre-packed or loose in bins so you can take the amount you require. Do not buy food that has lots of raisins and fruit in it as these can cause digestive problems such as diarrhoea and the high sugar content of the fruit can lead to dental disease and obesity.

Pellet or nugget food

These are hard blocks of food with all the ingredients needed packed into one chunk. This means the hamster cannot choose to feed selectively. This type of food is less common nowadays and has been replaced by the mixes.

Fresh food

Hamsters need to have fresh food once or twice a week at least. Remember you do not need to give much, the equivalent of an inch or so (2-3 cm) of dandelion leaf or a thin slice of carrot is plenty. Fresh herbs, such as parsley, clover and dandelion, grass, bits of apple, carrot, broccoli or grape will be much appreciated.

Avoid giving your hamster citrus fruits as these can cause sores on its mouth. Lettuce, spinach, buttercups, privet, ragwort, bluebells and pineapple should not be given to your hamster, nor any ornamental plants or flowers.

Do not feed grass cuttings from the lawn mower. Give picked grass only.

When giving any fresh food to your pet it is important to make sure it is rinsed well under cold water to clean away any dirt.

You should never feed any fruit or vegetable that is over or under-ripe or that is wilting, as this is not healthy for your hamster. A good rule of thumb to follow is: would you eat it? If not, then do not feed it to your pet.

Never collect fresh plants from the side of the road or from areas that have been, or are likely to have been, sprayed with pesticides as this will be harmful to your hamster.

Meat

Hamsters need meat protein in their diet. This is already in the better commercial diets, but your hamster will enjoy a little bird 'insect food' added to its dinner, the occasional mealworm, a small piece of plain, cooked chicken and even a bit of boiled or scrambled egg.

With both fresh food and meat, only give a small amount at a time. If you give too much and your hamster hoards it away it will quickly go bad and may cause your pet to become ill.

Treats

Pet shops now sell a range of treats for pet rodents, including hamsters. The best ones to use as treats are those that contain natural ingredients. Some can be hidden in their bedding, or hanging sticks and sprays of millet (often used for budgies) can be attached to the cage bars.

Do not give your pet human chocolate, crisps or salted nuts as these are very harmful to hamsters and will make them ill. Pet shops sell special pet chocolate and yogurt drops. These should be given as extra special treats as they are not very healthy for your pet. Likewise treats that are covered in honey or sticky sweet coatings should only be given sparingly. Hamsters can suffer from painful dental problems and also can get fat and suffer from heart disease or diabetes.

A treat is a treat, not part of the hamster's normal daily diet. Use them when you are playing with or training your hamster as a way to bond with him.

How much?

While it is normal for a hamster to hoard excess food, this hoard should not be large – if it is, you are feeding your pet too much. Weigh your pet regularly to ensure he is not putting on weight (once he is adult). If he is, then you are feeding it either too much, or, more likely, too many sugary treats.

Hamster care

Looking after your hamster means you need to keep its house clean and watch out for health problems. Cleaning out the cage might not be the most fun aspect of owning a hamster, but it is very rewarding when you watch your pet enjoy his freshly clean, comfortable surroundings and making his new bed. If the hamster is a pet for a child then remember you must ensure he is properly fed and the cage cleaned. It is important that an adult does the routine weekly health checks to ensure nothing is missed.

Hamsters are naturally extremely clean animals. They keep their home very tidy, remaking their bed every night by moving out any soiled bedding and they also check their food stores to remove any food that is decomposing. In addition a hamster leaves scent around its home. This acts as a territory marker, defining its property and making it feel safe, as well as warning others that they are entering its home. These fastidious hamster habits mean that the cage only needs to be lightly cleaned on a weekly basis with a more thorough clean every month.

Daily tasks

Refill the water-bottle with fresh water.

- Remove any wet bedding.

- Handle your hamster and give it an opportunity to explore in its play pen or exercise ball, and maybe do some training!

- Check your hamster's bottom to ensure it is clean.

See the 'Health' section for more information on checks.

Weekly tasks

Confine your hamster to a second holding cage, its play pen or exercise ball – somewhere it will be safe while you clean out its cage.

Remove all the toys, bowls and other objects in the cage. Remove all bedding and put some of it to one side. Throw the rest away.

Brush the cage out thoroughly with a stiff cleaning brush, and then give the floor of the cage a light spray with an 'animal friendly' disinfectant. Do not use any household cleaning products as these may be toxic to your pet.

Put in the new bedding and the bit of old bedding that you kept to one side. This means your hamster will feel safer when you return him to his home as he will have a familiar scent that he will recognise.

- Clean and fill the water bottle.

- Give your hamster an all-over health check – see Health section.

- Weigh your hamster to check he is not losing or gaining weight. Use household cooking scales for this, but do make sure your hamster does not fall out of the scale dish and hurt itself.

Monthly tasks

Once a month it is worth giving your hamster's cage a full clean. Follow the routine as described for the weekly clean, but wash down all the bars, shelving and your hamster's 'sleeping house' in a small animal safe disinfectant and rinse thoroughly with clean warm water. Do make sure everything is completely dry before putting in the new bedding (and some old bedding) and returning your hamster to its home.

Grooming

The amount of grooming each hamster needs depends on coat length. All hamsters can be groomed weekly. Long haired hamsters will need to be brushed more frequently to ensure the fur does not get tangled and matted. Grooming is a good way of bonding with your pet and helps keep the coat and underlying skin healthy. It also enables you to check for any problems. hamsters will groom themselves with great enthusiasm and are so flexible that they can reach all of their body. As hamsters get old they may become more stiff and will appreciate some gentle assistance in keeping their coat in tip-top condition.

There are several suitable brushes that can be used for your hamster, including a finger brush. This is a small rubber brush that fits on your finger like a thimble. Always brush the coat in the direction the hair lies.

If your hamster has long hair, ensure you hold the hair below the knot and gently ease the knot with small flicks of the brush. Do not tug, wrench or pull too hard or you may pull the hair out from the skin or even tear the skin. If the knot or tangle is not being moved easily, cut it away with a pair of curved surgical scissors. This needs to be done VERY carefully as hamsters can wriggle and squirm and it is very easy to cut the skin underneath. If in doubt contact your vet or an experienced hamster owner who may be able to do this for you.

Start grooming from an early age, perhaps when the hamster is enjoying a tasty treat, so that it learns to relax and enjoy the attention.

Bathing

You should only bathe your hamster if it is absolutely necessary. Hamsters lose heat very rapidly and if wet they can very quickly have a dangerously low body temperature. Most hamsters will never need a bath, and you certainly should not give them one just for fun.

If you do need to bathe your pet you will need a plastic bowl, a very soft, small hand towel, some small animal shampoo, available from your pet store, and a bowl of clean, tepid water to rinse your pet. Put a small amount of cool, tepid water, in the bowl. Remember not to make the water hot; what you may feel as warm may be far too hot for your hamster. You only need just enough to cover your hamster's legs. Gently put your hamster in the water and cup it with one hand. Lightly flick water over it with the other, avoiding the nose and eyes.

Once the coat is wet, gently massage in a small amount of the shampoo using a finger, but avoid the head, eyes and ears! Then you will need to rinse your pet's coat using the water in which it is standing and a final rinse or two with the clean water in the other bowl. Follow the same method as when you started to wet the coat. Rinse the coat clean, so all the soap suds have gone and the water runs clear from the coat.

You now need to dry your hamster. Do this using the towel and the tips of your fingers. Be very gentle, but do make sure your pet is completely dry. Expect to get bitten!! Having a bath is not an experience your hamster will enjoy, but will find very stressful.

Return your hamster to its cage, making sure there is lots of bedding for him to snuggle into. Then leave him in peace!

Hamster behaviour

One of the most rewarding things about owning a pet is learning to understand what it is thinking or feeling. You can learn a lot about what your hamster is saying to you by listening to the sounds it makes and observing its body postures.

Listen to your hamster

As solitary animals, hamsters are not very chatty
and make few noises that we can hear. They do make
sounds in the ultrasonic range, 20 – 60 KHz, but this is
way beyond our range of hearing. However, there are
a couple of sounds you may hear your hamster make.

Cackle

This is sound that hamsters use when they are
defending their home. Usually this is only made
when they see another hamster, but if your pet
is worried it may use the same noise to tell you it
wants to be left alone.

Teeth chattering

Again, this sound means 'go away', and is usually
used by males. If the other animal does not go away,
fighting is likely to ensue.

Squawk

If your hamster squawks it is telling you it is either
very frightened or in pain!

Watch your hamster

Scent rubbing

Being a solitary animal that is active in the dark of the night, the hamster's main form of communication is through scent – smells that we humans are unable to detect, let alone interpret. However, they clearly mean a lot to your hamster and you can watch him leaving messages all over the place. Syrian hamsters have scent glands on both flanks. These can be wet or greasy looking, and show as slightly darker patches. They are more obvious on male hamsters than females.

You will see your hamster arch its back and rub its flank on the walls of its cage and other vertical surfaces. It also will roll on its side to leave scent on the ground and on objects in its cage.

Happy hamster

Inquisitive

When your hamster is curious he will stand up on its back legs, with his front paws relaxed and drooping. It may have been a sound or a smell that caught his attention, such as your arrival, and it will turn to face the direction of your approach.

He may even climb up on to something so he can be a bit higher and thus see, hear and smell even better.

Curious but cautious

Hamsters are curious creatures, but sensibly are also cautious about any new thing they come across; after all, it may be dangerous.

When your hamster is investigating its world it will walk with a staggered gait that is made up of small, stiff movements, while rocking back and forth, ready to run if need be.

Annoyed hamster

Sitting back and 'bearing'

A hamster that is sitting back on its hind legs
looking like a miniature bear (hence the name of this
position) may look like he is smiling and ready for a
game. In fact, he is saying the direct opposite! This
position is a hamster's way of saying 'leave me alone
or I will attack'.

Ears pinned back

If your hamster's ears are pinned back against his
head, he is saying he wishes to be left alone. This is
the usual position of the ears when the hamster is
asleep... it is his 'Do not disturb' sign! If you wake
your hamster, wait until those ears are upright and
your pet is fully awake and ready to interact with you.

Frightened hamster

Freezing

When a hamster suddenly stops what he is doing and
'freezes on the spot' it means he has heard, seen or
smelt something unusual and scary. He is frightened.
This is usually followed by running back to a safe
shelter.

Playing dead

If your hamster lies absolutely still, usually on his back, he is extremely frightened. He is trying to pretend to be dead and thus of no interest to a predator.

If you see your hamster do this, leave him alone for 24 hours to recover. Think about what might have caused him to have been so very frightened. It may have been a loud noise, a sudden bright light, or being chased and grabbed. Try to avoid the situation occurring again.

Rolling on his back

If you startle your pet, for example by trying to pick him up when he is not fully awake, he may roll over on his back, kick and bite. While freezing and running away are the hamster's main form of self-defence, kicking and biting is another way of defending himself from what he perceives as a danger.

Unhappy hamster

Bar gnawing

You may see your hamster repeatedly gnawing at the bars of his cage, often for long periods at a time. This behaviour is a sign of an animal that is stressed, and a hamster may be so stressed that it does not stop even if he has made his nose and mouth sore, or damaged his teeth.

The common cause of this behaviour is boredom, meaning the hamster does not have enough space and / or things to do. Other causes include the cage being in a part of the house that is too brightly lit or too noisy.

You should try giving your pet more space and things to do and think carefully whether where you have put its cage in the most suitable place.

Health

Healthy hamsters can live up to two years. Handling your pet every day and performing regular health checks will help you pick up on the early signs of ill health and take action quickly to treat ailments before they become too serious. This is best done while handling your pet in the normal way. You should do any examinations as part of your grooming and regular play.

Weigh your hamster on a regular basis and remember to keep a record. Weight loss is often the first sign of ill health in a hamster.

You should know how your pet behaves while healthy. A sudden change in his normal pattern of behaviour can also indicate ill health, such as a change in eating habits, hiding more or becoming aggressive.

Hamsters are prey animals and are very good at disguising signs of illness and pain, so familiarity with your own pet is vital. It is important that you contact a vet as soon as possible if you have any concerns about your hamster's health. This section gives some of the more common problems that hamsters can suffer from.

Accidents, injuries or illness can occur and in the first instance a vet should be contacted to arrange treatment. But, in the time between the discovery of a problem and reaching the surgery, you are responsible for providing the best care you can.

Wounds & mishaps

Hamsters are active, inquisitive, short-sighted and so easily frightened that they may get injured when investigating their world or hurt themselves when trying to run away from something that has scared them.

Stress is often the underlying cause of wounds and bald patches on the nose, or around the lips. These can become inflamed, red or even bleeding due to bar rubbing. Your pet should be seen by the vet, and you should consider what stressors may be causing the problem.

Most minor grazes can be treated by being gently cleaned, using a cotton bud dipped in salty water (tap water and rock salt). However more serious injuries such as cuts must be looked at and treated by a veterinary surgeon as soon as possible to prevent infection and abscesses. Try and keep the wound as clean as possible until you go to the vet.

Hamsters have very fine bones which can easily fracture, including their skull. Blood in the nose or ears, could mean your pet has hurt its head badly. If you believe your pet has suffered a broken or fractured bone, or if you see blood in the urine, phone your vet immediately. Your vet may advise you to bring your pet in as soon as possible for stabilisation and pain relief. In the meantime keep it in a darkened and quiet area. It will feel more safe and relaxed in a dark enclosed space, such as its travelling box lined with soft bedding.

Teeth

Keep a close check on your hamster's teeth to make sure they do not grow too long or are mis-aligned. This can indicate a variety of possible problems, including inadequate diet, fractured teeth from a fall, abscesses or some other illness. If your hamster is having difficulty eating (this is one reason to check its weight weekly), you need to take it to the vet.

Be warned, overgrown teeth can lead to serious and even fatal problems for hamsters. The chance of your pet developing teeth problems is much less if it is fed correctly and has lots of suitable toys.

Nails

In the wild a hamster keeps its nails in trim by running and digging. A pet hamster's nails may grow too long, which will make moving very uncomfortable as the nails can curve over and dig into the bottom of the feet.

Providing your hamster with a digging pit will help keep his nails in good condition and give him a lot of fun. If your hamster's nails are overgrown then they will need to be trimmed. It is advised that you have them trimmed by the vet or an experienced hamster keeper who has done the task before.

Bumble foot

This is an extremely painful condition and is characterised by the feet being swollen and blistered, which can turn into open pressure sores. The infection can spread to the bones of the feet and if you see such signs on the feet of your hamster then you must take him to the vet as soon as you can.

A major cause of bumble foot is keeping hamsters on mesh floors rather than flat floors, or on damp, dirty bedding.

Wet tail

This is a secondary bacterial infection that occurs and takes hold when the hamster is already unwell. It is commonly triggered by stress – for example, transportation to the shop or new home, or excessive handling of a new hamster before he has settled in. Another cause is diet, typically too much fruit and vegetables.

Wet tail causes serious diarrhoea and the hamster can rapidly dehydrate, causing life-threatening loss of fluids and salts. The obvious symptoms are clumped greasy hair around the rump area with a strong sickly-sweet smell. The hamster will become very lethargic and withdrawn and the rest of his coat will look and feel greasy and stand on end.

In the later stages, the hamster's eyes look dull and sunken and the skin looses its elasticity. Such a degree of dehydration may cause further problems, such as kidney disease. All this can happen very quickly. The first 24 hours are the most important, so getting veterinary treatment is vital in the early stages.

Cleanliness is extremely important. Clean the cage at once, completely, and replace all bedding materials. Remove your pet's toys to reduce the places that the bacteria may grow. It may help to put a little millet spray and chopped peanuts into a food bowl with a little 'canary egg food' to help thicken up the stools. Sick hamsters may be so weakened that they will not drink from their bottle, so put a little juicy cucumber in the cage for them to nibble.

Hair loss

If your hamster has hair loss and is scratching a lot, he probably has a parasite infestation such as skin mites. Bald patches can also indicate other problems, so take your hamster to the vet.

Impacted pouches/ facial lumps

Sometimes hamsters try to put too much into their pouches or they struggle to remove items in them. Most commonly this is bedding material. This will have to be removed by you, an experienced hamster handler or a vet. If, after closer examination, it is not the cheek pouches that are causing the swelling it may be a tooth abscess or a tumour that will need urgent veterinary treatment.

Appearing dead/ hibernation

In the wild a hamster will hibernate during colder weather. If the ambient temperature falls to around 5°C (41°F) or lower then the hamster may enter a state of torpor – hibernation. With central heating it is unusual for the room temperature to fall so low, but it can happen. Certainly it was more common in the past, and it is sad to think that many a healthy, hibernating hamster has been mistakenly thought of as dead and been buried prematurely.

If you think that your hamster is hibernating, place it on to a warm towel in an open-top deep box – in his cage so he cannot accidentally get out and get lost. Put it into an airing cupboard or warm room where he can gently come round. Check on him periodically to ensure all is well.

If your hamster is sluggish and unresponsive and has not been exposed to cold, then he is ill and you should seek veterinary advice.

Twirling

This is when a hamster spins or walks in circles, over and over. If seen in a very young hamster it is possible he had brain damage from birth. In older animals, it may be the result of a middle ear infection or brain damage from a stroke or tumour.

It may also be, like bar biting, a behaviour that indicates a psychological problem, namely a stressed or bored hamster.

Hamster medicine

Veterinary knowledge of hamsters has increased hugely over the last few years and there is now much more that can be done for your pet. However, unlike cat and dog medicine which all veterinary surgeons know a lot about, hamsters are a specialist subject and it is worth finding a vet who is interested in them and their treatment.

Know your
pet hamster

Scientific name	Mesocricetus auratus
Group order	Rodentia
Breeding age	Males 3- 4 weeks; Females 3- 4 weeks
Gestation	16 days
Litter size	1- 11 (average 3- 4)
Birth weight	2 g (0.1 oz)
Birth type	Hairless, ears and eyes closed
Eyes open	15 days
Weaning	28- 30 days
Adult weight	80- 150 g (3- 5 ozs), males are smaller than females

Sources of further information

Orr, J and Lewin, T 2005 Getting Started: clicking with your rabbit Karen Pryor Publications – Gives excellent advice on how to train rabbits... which can also be applied to hamsters.

Websites

www.clickerbunny.com/clickercritterarticles.html - further information on training your hamster and other small pets.

www.hamsters-uk.org The National Hamster Club of the UK welcomes members from around the world.

Weights & measures

If you prefer your units in pounds and inches, you can use this conversion chart:

Length in inches	Length in cm	Weight in kg	Weight in lb
1	2.5	0.5	1.1
2	5.1	0.7	1.5
3	7.6	1	2.2
4	10.2	1.5	3.3
5	12.7	2	4.4
8	20.3	3	6.6
10	25.4	4	8.8
15	38.1	5	11

Measurements rounded to 1 decimal place.